Please Tell!

A Child's Story About Sexual Abuse

Written and Illustrated By
Jessie

With a Foreword by Sandra Hewitt, Ph.D.

HAZELDEN®

First published August 1991.

ISBN 13: 978-0-89486-776-7

Library of Congress Catalog Card Number: 91-72598

Printed in the United States of America.

About the author:

Jessie was nine when she first wrote *Please Tell!* and eleven when she revised and illustrated it. Jessie enjoys crafts, jazz dancing, and gymnastics, and hopes to be a dance teacher or perhaps a marine biologist one day. About her book Jessie says, ''I just want *Please Tell!* to help people as much as it helped me to write it.''

Foreword

By Sandra Hewitt, Ph.D.

One of the central dynamics of child sexual abuse is secrecy: children are told by their abusers not to tell. When secrecy exists, pain is borne alone. This isolation compounds the pain and confusion caused by abuse.

Child therapists, child protection workers, teachers, victim witness assistants, counselors, and even parents will find that this book can be used to speak directly to children on several levels.

First, for children who have been abused, this book offers affirmation for their disclosure, as well as the knowledge that they are not alone, that this has happened to someone else too. Often the treatment of young children is done individually. These children aren't able to get the support of other abused children. Children who have been sexually abused feel stigmatized. They often feel that because something bad happened to them, they must be bad or weird. Learning that they are not alone can help soften this sense of shame and isolation. Jessie's words and pictures let other children know they are not alone, and that it is good to tell.

On a second level, this book can be used by professionals who evaluate sexual abuse. Care must be taken not to contaminate the information a child gives during evaluation of the abuse, but much more often than being told what *to* say, children are told what *not* to say—don't tell about the abuse. When a child is censured or fearful, Jessie's direct child-to-child words can speak as no adult can. They carry the message *It's okay to tell. Help can come when you tell.*

On a third level, sexual abuse prevention trainers may find this book helpful to share as they teach children about sexual abuse and how to deal with it. Jessie depicts a child's courage to tell, and the help that comes afterward. In doing this, she lets other children understand how it feels when abuse happens. Because many children are afraid to tell their friends they have been abused, they live with their pain and shame alone. Jessie's words help share the feelings and needs of abused children in a way that lets other children understand better how to relate to the abused child's needs.

Not all sexual abuse cases result in the kind of effective resolution that Jessie experienced. But even with cases in which a child's statements are slow to be believed and supported, Jessie's story can add a sense of hope for what should be, and the knowledge that the child protection system can work for children.

Children can talk to children in a way adults can't. Simple, direct, and from the heart, Jessie's message can help give children the permission and the courage to deal with sexual abuse.

Sandra Hewitt, Ph.D., is the author of literature on childhood sexual abuse. Employed by River City Mental Health Clinic, St. Paul, Minnesota, Hewitt writes and does research and is a frequent lecturer across the country.

To my cousins, who went through it with me.

Dear friends everywhere,

I was hurt by someone I loved
and trusted, when I was four.

He was my uncle and my godfather.

He made me do things
I didn't want to do at all!
He hurt my arms and legs
and places that are private on my body.

I told him NO!
He didn't listen.

He had an evil smile.
It seemed like his eyes
almost turned red.

For a while I never told because
he said he would do awful things,
like beat me or my mom or dad,
or do to my baby sister what he did to me.

He said if I told,
bad men would take me away
and cut off all my hair.

After a while,
something didn't seem right.

With all my fingers crossed, I told,
getting ready for a mad face from Mom and Dad.

When I looked up,
all I saw was that Mom and Dad loved me.

They were glad I told.

My mom and dad took me to see
some ladies with dolls.
I pretended a girl doll was me
and a boy doll was my uncle.
I used dolls to show them what he did to me.

The police went to see my uncle.

He never hurt me again,
and he never did the things he said he would do.

Now I am nine.
I still have the terrible memory
in my head.
The trouble is getting over it.

Mommy and me thought of a way
to get the nightmares out of my head
when I'm thinking of him—and it works!

I pretend that I can have
anything I wish for. Then I think of what I would give
everyone in my family.

Soon the scary memory vanishes
from my head. Finally I fall asleep.

But a woman named Susan
helped me even more.

She has a special job.
She helps children with their problems
or fears. She's called a psychologist.
She helped me understand what happened.
I learned what happened to me is called abuse.

You don't have to be scared to tell a psychologist
about how you were abused.
He or she is trained to help you,
and they will—trust me!

If you can't see a psychologist,
just tell someone, like a teacher,
a friend, or someone special.

Keep telling until someone helps you.
You don't have to live in a bad dream anymore.

When I'm around men, I feel scared
and embarrassed because of what happened
to my body. If you have been abused,
don't worry. It's okay if you feel
that way too.

Now I feel lots of anger.
But I know it's not everyday angry feelings.
I think it's because of my uncle.

So what I do is throw my pillow around
and scream into it. That makes me feel much better.

Some things that helped me are
hugs from Mom and Dad,
lots of love, and talking about my feelings.

I know that being abused will always be
a sad memory in my heart.
But with Susan's help I can get over it
and still enjoy the fun things
in my life.

I felt like I did something very wrong.
But now I understand that I did something very right
and HE did something very wrong.

If this happens to you, tell right away.

Ask to see a psychologist,
or someone special.
Talk to someone who knows how to help
children who have been abused.

I know what it feels like
when a grown-up confuses you.
You don't feel safe anywhere.

So don't be afraid to tell people
you need help with your feelings.
I got help, and you can too!

Your friend,

Jessie

**Here are some people you could talk to
if you have been abused:**

Mom or Dad

Aunt or Uncle

Grandmother or Grandfather

Adult Friend

Family Doctor

School Counselor

School Psychologist

Teacher

Principal

Police (dial 911)

Social Services Agency

Family Services Agency

Children's Hospital

Sometimes the people you tell don't believe you.
Keep telling until someone helps you.
Jessie got help, and you will too.